THE GOOD SAMARITAN

WRITTEN AND ILLUSTRATED BY
ABBEY HILL

To my Husband,
Son, and Future Children -
may God bless your lives
with the holiness of His teachings.

Special thanks to my mentor,
guide, and mother.

The Good Samaritan
Copyright © 2025 by Abbey Hill

Published by Lucid Books in Houston, TX
www.LucidBooks.com

All rights reserved. No part of this publication may be reproduced, stored in a retrieval system, or transmitted in any form by any means, electronic, mechanical, photocopy, recording, or otherwise, without the prior permission of the publisher, except as provided for by USA copyright law.

Scripture quotations been taken from the Christian Standard Bible®, Copyright © 2017 by Holman Bible Publishers. Used by permission. Christian Standard Bible® and CSB® are federally registered trademarks of Holman Bible Publishers.

ISBN: 978-1-63296-795-4 (hardback)
ISBN: 978-1-63296-796-1 (paperback)
eISBN: 978-1-63296-797-8

Special Sales: Most Lucid Books titles are available in special quantity discounts. Custom imprinting or excerpting can also be done to fit special needs. Contact Lucid Books at Info@LucidBooks.com.

What is a Parable?

A **PARABLE** is a short story
that teaches a lesson.

It's like a simple tale that helps us
understand something important,
like being kind or making good choices.

Jesus taught using parables
because He taught about things
that were hard to understand.

In the parable of The Good Samaritan,
a man asks Jesus,

"Who is my neighbor?"

Jesus tells a story that will help the man
understand not only who our neighbors are,
but also how to treat them the way God
wants us to treat them.

LUKE 10:29-36

A man was going down from Jerusalem to Jericho and fell into the hands of robbers.

They stripped him,
beat him up,
and fled,
leaving him half dead.

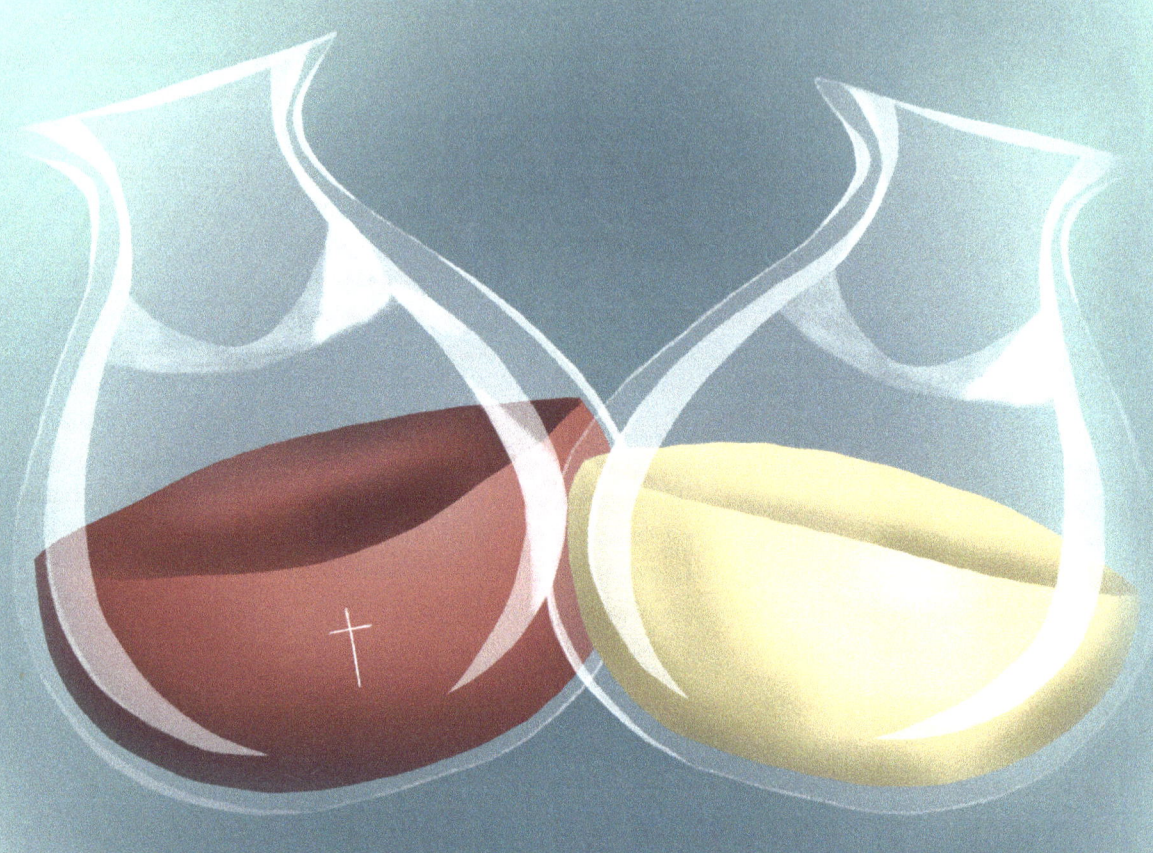

He went over to him and bandaged his wounds,
pouring on olive oil and wine.

Then he put him on his own animal, brought him to an inn, and took care of him.

The next day he took out two denarii, gave them to the innkeeper, and said,

"Take care of him. When I come back I'll reimburse you for whatever extra you spend."

"Which of these three do you think proved to be a neighbor to the man who fell into the hands of the robbers?"

When the man in the parable is hurt, many people pass by and choose not to help him.

The Samaritan not only helps get the man to shelter, but also pays for his stay and any expense the man had.

Jesus teaches us that we should help everyone, no matter who they are.

WE ARE ALL GOD'S CHILDREN.
We are all made in His image.

This means when someone needs help, we are supposed to be like the Samaritan and help them to the best of our ability.

Helping doesn't always mean fixing big problems. We can make a Christ-like impact on the people in our daily lives just by helping in small ways.

Who can I help this week
to be more like the Samaritan?

How have I been a
good neighbor this week?

When could I have been
a better neighbor this week?

What is something I can do
to be more like the Samaritan?

www.ingramcontent.com/pod-product-compliance
Lightning Source LLC
Chambersburg PA
CBHW061418090426
42743CB00023B/3487